FROM DOORMAT TO
DELIGHTFUL

*The Art of Transforming Toxic Relationships or
Leaving Them*

Stella Joseph

Dedication

To everyone who seeks the courage to be free and live a peaceful, healthy relationship.

Contents

Introduction

The phone rang, its shrill tone shattering the fragile peace I'd carefully constructed around myself. My heart pounded in my chest, a familiar drumbeat of dread accompanying the caller ID that flashed across the screen: "John."

I hesitated, my finger hovering over the answer button. A war raged within me. One part of me, the stronger, wiser part, whispered, "Don't answer. You know what this will be." But the other part, the part that had been conditioned over years of emotional manipulation, couldn't resist the siren call of his voice. I answered.

His words poured out in a torrent of accusations, insults, and self-pity. I listened, nodding dumbly, my stomach churning with a mix of guilt and resentment. He needed me, he said. I was the only one who understood him. I was his lifeline. And like a puppet on a string, I danced to his tune, my own needs and desires fading into the background.

That night, after hanging up the phone, I sat on the edge of my bed, tears streaming down my face. I felt empty, exhausted, and utterly worthless. In that moment, I finally saw myself for what I had become: a doormat.

It hadn't happened overnight. The transformation had been subtle, insidious. Like a slow-growing vine, John's toxicity had wrapped itself around me, choking the life out of my spirit. At first, I'd been drawn to his intensity, his passionate nature. He'd swept me off my feet, showering me with affection and attention. But over time, the compliments turned to criticisms, the affection to control. I walked on eggshells, terrified of saying or doing anything that might trigger his anger. I became an expert at anticipating his every need, putting his happiness above my own.

And the more I gave, the more he took.

Being a doormat is not about being kind or compassionate. It's about sacrificing your own well-being to please someone else. It's about putting up with disrespect, manipulation, and even abuse, all in the name of "love." It's a pattern of behavior that often stems from low self-esteem, a fear of conflict, or a deep-seated need to be needed.

The pitfalls of being a doormat are many. You lose yourself in the relationship, your own needs and desires becoming secondary to your partner's. You become a prisoner of your own fear, afraid to speak up or stand up for yourself. You give and give until you have nothing left to give, leaving you feeling depleted and resentful. And worst of all, you teach others how to treat you by tolerating their bad behavior.

But here's the good news: You don't have to live like this. You can break free from the doormat trap and reclaim your power. You can learn to set healthy boundaries, communicate your needs, and prioritize your own well-being. You can discover your own worth and create a life filled with joy, love, and respect.

That's what this book is all about. It's a guide to transforming toxic relationships or, if necessary, leaving them. It's about rediscovering your own strength, setting healthy boundaries, and reclaiming your life. It's about learning to love yourself first and foremost, so that you can attract healthy, fulfilling relationships into your life.

This journey won't be easy. It will require courage, honesty, and a willingness to face some uncomfortable truths. But I promise you, it will be worth it. Because on the other side of the doormat trap lies a life of freedom, joy, and authentic connection.

In the following chapters, we'll explore the signs of a toxic relationship, the different types of toxic people, and the impact they can have on your life. We'll delve into the psychology of being a doormat, uncovering the root causes of this behavior and the ways it can sabotage your happiness. We'll learn how to set healthy boundaries, communicate effectively, and deal with resistance and backlash. We'll talk about when and how to leave a toxic relationship, and how to heal and recover from the emotional trauma. And finally, we'll explore how to build healthy, fulfilling relationships based on mutual respect, trust, and love.

This book is not a quick fix. It's a journey of self-discovery, healing, and transformation. But if you're ready to break free from the doormat trap and create a life you love, then this book is for you.

Welcome to the beginning of your journey from doormat to delightful. It's time to reclaim your power and step into your full potential.

Part I: Recognizing and Understanding Toxicity

Chapter 1: The Anatomy of a Toxic Relationship

Imagine a vibrant flowerbed, each bloom representing a relationship in your life. Some flowers stand tall, their colors radiant, their scent intoxicating. These are the healthy relationships that nourish and uplift you. But nestled among them, you might spot a few wilting blossoms, their petals drooping, their colors dull. These are the toxic relationships, the ones that drain your energy, dim your light, and leave you feeling depleted.

Toxic relationships aren't always easy to identify. They often begin with a whirlwind of passion and excitement, making it difficult to see the warning signs lurking beneath the surface. But like a slow-acting poison, their toxic effects gradually seep into your life, eroding your self-esteem, your joy, and your very sense of self.

So, what exactly makes a relationship toxic? It's not just about occasional disagreements or misunderstandings. Healthy relationships have their share of ups and downs. But toxic relationships are characterized by a persistent pattern of unhealthy behaviors and dynamics that create a toxic environment.

One of the hallmarks of a toxic relationship is a lack of respect. Your partner may belittle your opinions, dismiss your feelings, or constantly criticize you. They may try to control your actions, isolate you from your friends and family, or make you feel guilty for pursuing your own interests. This constant barrage of negativity can leave you feeling insecure, worthless, and doubting your own sanity.

Another key characteristic of a toxic relationship is a power imbalance. One partner may dominate the other, making all the decisions, controlling the finances, or dictating the terms of the relationship. This can leave the other partner feeling powerless, voiceless, and trapped.

Emotional manipulation is another common tactic used in toxic relationships. Your partner may use guilt trips, silent treatment, or gaslighting to get their way. They may play the victim, blaming you for their problems, or twist your words to make you feel like you're the one at fault. This can leave you feeling confused, frustrated, and questioning your own reality.

In addition to these emotional tactics, physical and verbal abuse are also clear signs of a toxic relationship. Any form of violence, whether it's hitting, pushing, or throwing objects, is unacceptable and should never be tolerated. Verbal abuse, such as name-calling, insults, or threats, is equally damaging and can leave deep emotional scars.

These are just a few of the red flags that signal a toxic relationship. Other warning signs include constant jealousy and possessiveness, a lack of trust and communication, and a feeling of walking on eggshells around your partner. If you find yourself constantly apologizing for your partner's behavior, making excuses for their actions, or feeling drained and unhappy in the relationship, these are all signs that you may be in a toxic situation.

It's important to remember that toxic relationships don't happen overnight. They often develop gradually, with subtle warning signs that are easy to miss or dismiss. The initial stages may be filled with passion and excitement, masking the underlying problems. But over time, the toxic behaviors become more frequent and intense, creating a cycle of emotional pain and turmoil.

Understanding how toxic relationships develop can help you spot the early warning signs and take steps to protect yourself. Often, these relationships begin with a seemingly perfect match. Your partner may shower you with attention and affection, making you feel special and loved. But as time goes on, their true colors start to show.

They may become increasingly critical, finding fault with everything you do. They may try to isolate you from your friends and family, making you dependent on them for emotional support. They may start to control your actions, dictating what you wear, who you see, and how you spend your time. These subtle shifts in behavior can be easy to overlook, especially if you're blinded by love or hope for the relationship.

Red Flags: Identifying Toxic Behaviors

Remember those wilting flowers in your relationship garden? They don't always announce their toxicity with a neon sign. Instead, they subtly display red flags, warning signs that something isn't quite right. These red flags may seem small at first, but over time, they can grow into a tangled mess of thorns, choking the life out of your happiness.

So, what are these red flags? They come in various forms, often disguised as love or concern. But beneath the surface, they reveal a toxic undercurrent that can erode your well-being. Here are a few common red flags to watch for:

1. **Constant Criticism:** Does your partner constantly criticize your appearance, your choices, or your personality? Do they make you feel like you're never good enough? This constant negativity can chip away at your self-esteem, leaving you feeling insecure and unworthy.

2. **Controlling Behavior:** Does your partner try to control who you see, what you wear, or how you spend your time? Do they get jealous or angry when you assert your independence? This controlling behavior can suffocate you, leaving you feeling trapped and powerless.

3. **Lack of Respect:** Does your partner dismiss your opinions, belittle your feelings, or make fun of your dreams? Do they talk down to you or interrupt you constantly? This lack of respect can make you feel invisible and unheard.

4. **Emotional Manipulation:** Does your partner use guilt trips, silent treatment, or gaslighting to get their way? Do they blame you for their problems or twist your words to make you feel like you're the one at fault? This emotional manipulation can leave you feeling confused, frustrated, and doubting your own reality.

5. **Isolation:** Does your partner try to isolate you from your friends and family? Do they discourage you from pursuing your own interests or hobbies? This isolation can leave you feeling lonely and dependent on your partner for everything.

6. **Physical or Verbal Abuse:** Does your partner ever hit, push, or shove you? Do they yell at you, call you names, or threaten you? Any form of violence, whether physical or verbal, is a major red flag and should never be tolerated.

These are just a few of the red flags that can signal a toxic relationship. If you notice any of these signs in your own relationship, it's important to take them seriously. Don't brush them off or make excuses for your partner's behavior. Trust your gut feeling and seek help if needed. Remember, you deserve to be in a healthy, loving relationship that nourishes and uplifts you.

The Doormat Mindset: How We Become Vulnerable

The roots of the "doormat mindset" often lie deep within us, shaped by our past experiences, cultural conditioning, and even our own personalities. We may have grown up in families where we were taught to prioritize others' needs above our own, to avoid conflict at all costs, or to believe that our worth was tied to our ability to please others. We may have been exposed to societal messages that reinforced these beliefs, telling us that being selfless and accommodating is the key to a successful relationship.

Over time, these messages can become ingrained in our subconscious, shaping the way we view ourselves and our relationships. We may start to believe that our own needs and desires are less important than our partner's, that we don't deserve to be treated with respect, or that we're not capable of standing up for ourselves. This can create a vicious cycle where we attract partners who take advantage of our willingness to please, further reinforcing our doormat tendencies.

Certain personality traits can also make us more vulnerable to the doormat mindset. People-pleasers, for instance, often have a strong desire to be liked and approved of, leading them to go to great lengths to avoid conflict or disappointment. Empathetic individuals may find it difficult to set boundaries because they feel deeply for others' pain and want to alleviate it, even at their own expense. And those with low self-esteem may believe that they don't deserve better treatment, making them more likely to tolerate disrespect and mistreatment.

Recognizing these vulnerabilities is the first step towards breaking free from the doormat mindset. By understanding how our past experiences, cultural conditioning, and personality traits have shaped our beliefs and behaviors, we can start to challenge these patterns and develop a healthier sense of self-worth. We can learn to set boundaries, communicate our needs assertively, and prioritize our own well-being. This process takes time and effort, but it is essential for creating healthy, fulfilling relationships based on mutual respect and love. Remember, you are not a doormat, but a beautiful flower deserving of care and nourishment.

Self-Reflection Questions

1. Do you often find yourself prioritizing your partner's needs above your own, even when it leaves you feeling depleted or resentful?

2. Have you noticed any red flags in your relationship, such as constant criticism, controlling behavior, or emotional manipulation?

3. Do you feel like you're walking on eggshells around your partner, afraid to express your true feelings or opinions?

4. Has your self-esteem suffered as a result of your relationship? Do you feel less confident or worthy than you used to?

5. Do you believe that you deserve to be treated with love, respect, and dignity in your relationship?

Transformative Exercises

1. **Red Flag Journal:** Keep a journal for one week and record any instances of red flag behavior from your partner. Reflect on how these behaviors made you feel and whether they are a recurring pattern.

2. **Self-Care Ritual:** Create a daily self-care ritual that nourishes your mind, body, and soul. This could include

activities like meditation, exercise, reading, spending time in nature, or enjoying a relaxing bath.

3. **Boundary Setting Practice:** Identify one area in your relationship where you need to set a boundary. Practice communicating this boundary clearly and assertively to your partner.

4. **Affirmation Mirror Work:** Stand in front of a mirror and repeat positive affirmations that affirm your self-worth and remind you of your strengths. For example, "I am worthy of love and respect," "I am strong and capable," or "I am enough."

5. **Gratitude Practice:** Each day, write down three things you are grateful for. This could include aspects of your relationship, your own qualities, or simple joys in your life. This practice can help shift your focus from negativity to positivity and cultivate a greater sense of appreciation for yourself and your life.

Chapter 2: Types of Toxic People

In the course of our interactions with people of distinct backgrounds, we encounter a diverse array of personalities, each with their own unique traits and quirks. While many bring joy and enrichment to our lives, others can leave a trail of emotional wreckage in their wake. These are the toxic individuals, the energy vampires, the master manipulators who thrive on control and chaos. Recognizing these toxic types is crucial for safeguarding your well-being and ensuring you don't fall prey to their destructive games.

One of the most notorious toxic personalities is the narcissist. These individuals possess an inflated sense of self-importance, crave constant admiration, and lack empathy for others. Their world revolves around their own needs and desires, and they have no qualms about exploiting others to achieve their goals. Narcissists often charm their way into relationships, showering their partners with attention and affection. However, this initial charm quickly fades, revealing a manipulative and controlling personality. They may belittle your accomplishments, gaslight your emotions, and isolate you from your support system. Their constant need for validation can leave you feeling emotionally drained and questioning your own worth.

Another toxic type to be wary of is the emotional manipulator. These individuals are skilled at playing with your emotions, using guilt, shame, and fear to control your behavior. They may feign helplessness or victimhood to elicit sympathy, or they may resort to silent treatment or passive-aggressive tactics to punish you for not complying with their wishes. Emotional manipulators often lack emotional maturity and have difficulty taking responsibility for their own actions. Their manipulative behavior can leave you feeling confused, anxious, and constantly walking on eggshells.

Controllers are yet another breed of toxic individuals who can wreak havoc on your life. These individuals have an insatiable need to control every aspect of your life, from your daily routines to your social interactions. They may criticize your choices, question your decisions, and even dictate what you wear or who you spend time with. Controllers often have a rigid view of the world and believe that their way is the only way. Their controlling behavior can stifle your individuality, erode your self-confidence, and leave you feeling trapped and suffocated.

Other toxic types of humans you may encounter are the chronic complainer, who constantly focuses on the negative and drains your energy with their endless grievances; the drama queen, who thrives on chaos and conflict, creating drama wherever they go; and the gossip monger, who spreads rumors and misinformation, causing unnecessary pain and division.

However, not everyone who exhibits these behaviors is necessarily toxic. We all have our moments of selfishness, insecurity, or need for control. However, toxic individuals consistently engage in these destructive patterns, causing significant harm to those around them. Recognizing these patterns is crucial for protecting yourself from their negative influence.

So, how can you spot these toxic individuals in your life? Pay attention to how they make you feel. Do you feel drained, anxious, or insecure after spending time with them? Do they constantly criticize, belittle, or manipulate you? Do they try to control your actions or isolate you from your support system? If so, these are all red flags that you may be dealing with a toxic person.

It's also important to observe their behavior towards others. Do they treat everyone with respect and kindness, or do they reserve their worst behavior for those closest to them? Do they have a history of unstable relationships or a pattern of leaving a trail of emotional wreckage in their wake? These are all important clues that can help you identify toxic individuals before they cause too much damage.

Narcissist: A Master of Manipulation

In the realm of toxic personalities, the narcissist reigns supreme as a master of manipulation. These individuals possess a grandiose sense of self-importance, an insatiable craving for admiration, and a complete lack of empathy for others. Their world revolves around their own needs and desires, and they will stop at nothing to get what they want, even if it means trampling on the feelings of those around them.

Narcissists are experts at charming their way into your life. They may shower you with compliments, attention, and affection, making you feel special and adored. But beware, this is just a facade, a carefully crafted mask designed to lure you into their web of manipulation. Once they have you hooked, their true colors begin to show.

Their compliments turn into criticisms, their affection into control. They may belittle your accomplishments, gaslight your emotions, and isolate you from your support system. They may play the victim, blaming you for their problems, or twist your words to make you feel like you're the one at fault. Their constant need for validation can leave you feeling emotionally drained, insecure, and questioning your own sanity.

One of the narcissist's most powerful weapons is gaslighting, a form of psychological manipulation that makes you doubt your own reality. They may deny things they said or did, accuse you of being overly sensitive or imagining things, or twist the truth to fit their own narrative. Over time, this constant manipulation can erode your self-confidence and leave you feeling confused and disoriented.

Another tactic narcissists use is projection, where they attribute their own negative traits and behaviors onto you. For example, if they are dishonest, they may accuse you of lying. If they are controlling, they may accuse you of being clingy or needy. This projection serves to deflect blame from themselves and further manipulate you into believing that you are the problem.

Narcissists are also skilled at playing the victim. They may exaggerate their own problems or create drama to garner sympathy and attention. They may even go so far as to fabricate stories or accuse others of wrongdoing to paint themselves in a positive light. This victim mentality allows them to avoid taking responsibility for their own actions and maintain their sense of superiority.

Breaking free from a narcissist's grasp can be incredibly challenging. They are masters of manipulation and will often use guilt, shame, and fear to keep you under their control. It's important to remember that you are not responsible for their behavior and that you deserve to be treated with respect and love. Seek support from trusted friends, family, or professionals who can help you navigate this difficult situation and reclaim your power.

The Emotional Vampire: Draining Your Energy

Emotional vampires are subtle predators, lurking in the shadows of our lives, ready to siphon off our energy and leave us feeling drained and depleted. They may not have fangs or capes, but their impact can be just as devastating. These individuals feed on our empathy, our compassion, and our willingness to listen. They are masters of emotional manipulation, drawing us into their dramas and leaving us feeling responsible for their happiness.

Identifying an emotional vampire can be tricky, as they often disguise their energy-draining tactics as cries for help or genuine sharing. You may find yourself listening to their endless complaints, their tales of woe, their never-ending dramas. They may constantly seek your advice, your support, your validation. And while it's natural to want to help a friend in need, spending time with an emotional vampire can leave you feeling emotionally exhausted and depleted.

Unlike healthy relationships, where there is a give-and-take of emotional support, interactions with emotional vampires are one-sided. They take, and take, and take, without offering anything in return. They may interrupt you when you try to share your own experiences, dismiss your concerns, or turn the conversation back to themselves. They may even make you feel guilty for not being able to meet their endless demands for attention and validation.

The emotional vampire's impact can be insidious. Over time, their constant negativity can wear you down, leaving you feeling drained, irritable, and even depressed. They may also create drama and conflict in your life, as their insatiable need for attention often leads to chaos and upheaval. It's important to recognize these signs and set healthy boundaries with emotional vampires, protecting your own energy and well-being. Remember, you are not responsible for their happiness, and you have the right to choose who you spend your time and energy with.

Self-Reflection Questions

1. Have you ever felt drained or emotionally exhausted after spending time with someone? Do certain individuals consistently leave you feeling this way?

2. Do you find yourself constantly giving advice, support, or validation to someone without receiving anything in return?

3. Have you ever been in a relationship where you felt like your partner was always the center of attention, and your needs were consistently overlooked?

4. Do you ever feel manipulated or controlled by someone's emotions, guilt trips, or passive-aggressive behavior?

5. Do you feel like you're constantly walking on eggshells around someone, afraid to say or do anything that might upset them?

Transformative Exercises

1. **Energy Audit:** After interacting with someone, take a moment to assess your energy levels. Do you feel energized and uplifted, or drained and depleted? Use this as a gauge to identify potential emotional vampires in your life.

2. **The Power of No:** Practice saying "no" to requests or demands that drain your energy or don't align with your values. Remember, you have the right to set boundaries and protect your well-being.

3. **Limit Exposure:** If you identify someone as an emotional vampire, limit your interactions with them. You don't have to cut them out of your life completely, but set boundaries on how much time and energy you invest in the relationship.

4. **Focus on Self-Care:** Prioritize activities that nourish your mind, body, and soul. This could include exercise, meditation, spending time in nature, or pursuing hobbies you enjoy. By taking care of yourself, you replenish your energy reserves and become less susceptible to emotional vampires.

5. **Seek Support:** Talk to a trusted friend, family member, or therapist about your experiences with emotional vampires. Their support and guidance can help you navigate these challenging relationships and protect your well-being.

Chapter 3: The Impact of Toxicity on Your Life

Let's paint a picture of a beautiful forest; the forest is teeming with life and energy. Each tree stands tall, its branches reaching towards the sky, its roots firmly anchored in the nourishing earth. Now picture a toxic spill seeping into the soil, poisoning the very foundation of this ecosystem. The once-thriving trees begin to wither, their leaves turning brown, their branches drooping. The vibrant ecosystem transforms into a barren wasteland, devoid of life and beauty.

This is a stark metaphor for the impact of toxicity on your life. A toxic relationship is like that poisonous spill, slowly but surely contaminating every aspect of your being. It starts with subtle changes, a gradual erosion of your self-esteem, your joy, your very sense of self. Over time, the effects become more pronounced, leaving you feeling emotionally drained, psychologically scarred, and even physically ill.

Emotionally, toxic relationships can leave you feeling like a shell of your former self. The constant criticism, manipulation, and gaslighting can erode your confidence and make you doubt your own worth. You may find yourself constantly second-guessing your decisions, apologizing for your feelings, and walking on eggshells around your partner. The emotional rollercoaster of highs and lows can leave you feeling anxious, depressed, and emotionally exhausted.

At this juncture, we should look at the stories individuals shared with me on how toxicity in their relationships had a toll on them even after leaving the toxic relationships.

One woman, Sarah, shared her experience of being in a toxic relationship with a narcissistic partner. She described feeling like she was constantly walking on eggshells, never knowing what version of her partner she would encounter each day. The constant criticism and belittling wore down her self-esteem, leaving her feeling worthless and inadequate. She started to isolate herself from friends and family, believing that she deserved the mistreatment she was receiving.

Psychologically, toxic relationships can leave lasting scars. The constant stress and anxiety can lead to a range of mental health issues, including depression, anxiety disorders, and post-traumatic stress disorder (PTSD). Studies have shown that individuals in toxic relationships are more likely to experience symptoms of depression and anxiety, and they may also have difficulty forming healthy relationships in the future.

John, a man who escaped a controlling and manipulative relationship, described the psychological toll it took on him. He constantly felt like he was walking on thin ice, afraid to say or do anything that might upset his partner. He developed severe anxiety and started having panic attacks. Even after leaving the relationship, he struggled with trust issues and found it difficult to open up to new people.

Physically, the impact of a toxic relationship can be just as devastating. The constant stress can wreak havoc on your body, leading to a weakened immune system, sleep problems, digestive issues, and even chronic pain. Studies have shown that individuals in toxic relationships are more likely to suffer from headaches, stomachaches, and other physical ailments.

Emily, a woman who endured years of emotional abuse, described the physical toll it took on her. She developed chronic migraines, insomnia, and stomach ulcers. She also experienced unexplained weight loss and hair loss. After leaving the relationship and seeking therapy, she was able to heal both emotionally and physically.

The impact of a toxic relationship can extend beyond the individual and affect their loved ones as well. Children who grow up in toxic environments are more likely to experience behavioral problems, emotional difficulties, and academic challenges. They may also be at increased risk of developing mental health issues later in life.

Friends and family members of those in toxic relationships often feel helpless and frustrated. They may witness the emotional and physical toll the relationship is taking on their loved one, but feel powerless to intervene. They may also experience their own emotional distress, as they worry about their loved one's safety and well-being.

It's important to remember that the effects of a toxic relationship are not always immediately apparent. The damage can be insidious, slowly eroding your self-esteem, your health, and your overall well-being. It's like a silent poison, gradually weakening your spirit and leaving you feeling trapped and powerless.

Emotional and Psychological Toll

The emotional and psychological scars inflicted by a toxic relationship can be as deep and lasting as any physical wound. They burrow into your soul, eroding your self-esteem, distorting your perception of reality, and leaving you feeling lost and broken. The constant barrage of criticism, manipulation, and emotional abuse can chip away at your confidence, making you doubt your own worth and abilities. You may start to believe the negative things your partner says about you, internalizing their toxic words as your own truth.

The psychological impact of a toxic relationship can manifest in various ways. You may experience anxiety, depression, or even post-traumatic stress disorder (PTSD). Sleepless nights, racing thoughts, and a constant sense of dread may become your new normal. The emotional rollercoaster of highs and lows can leave you feeling emotionally exhausted and unable to cope with everyday challenges.

One of the most insidious effects of a toxic relationship is the loss of self. As you try to please your partner and avoid conflict, you may start to neglect your own needs and desires. Your hobbies, passions, and even your friendships may fall by the wayside as you become increasingly consumed by the toxic dynamic of the relationship. You may even start to lose sight of who you are as an individual, your identity becoming intertwined with your partner's.

The psychological scars of a toxic relationship can also impact your future relationships. You may find it difficult to trust new people, fearing that they will hurt you in the same way. You may also struggle with intimacy and vulnerability, afraid to open up and let someone else in. It's important to remember that healing from these emotional wounds takes time and effort. Seeking professional help, such as therapy or counseling, can be invaluable in this process.

Physical Health Consequences

The relentless stress and emotional turmoil of a toxic relationship can wreak havoc on your body, manifesting in a myriad of physical ailments. It's as if the poison seeping into your soul also finds its way into your cells, disrupting the delicate balance of your physical well-being.

The constant state of anxiety and hypervigilance can trigger a cascade of stress hormones, leading to elevated blood pressure, increased heart rate, and a weakened immune system. You may find yourself falling ill more frequently, unable to shake off even the most minor of colds or infections. Chronic headaches, stomachaches, and fatigue may become your unwelcome companions, as your body struggles to cope with the emotional burden you carry.

Sleep often becomes elusive in a toxic relationship. The worries and anxieties swirling in your mind may keep you tossing and turning at night, leaving you feeling exhausted and depleted in the morning. This lack of restorative sleep further compromises your immune system, making you more susceptible to illness and disease.

The physical toll of a toxic relationship can extend beyond these immediate symptoms. Over time, the chronic stress can increase your risk of developing more serious health conditions, such as heart disease, stroke, and even certain types of cancer. The toll on your digestive system can manifest as irritable bowel syndrome (IBS), ulcers, or other gastrointestinal problems. Even your skin, a reflection of your inner health, may bear the brunt of the emotional turmoil, with breakouts, rashes, or other skin conditions flaring up.

It's important to recognize that these physical symptoms are not merely coincidences. They are the body's way of signaling that something is amiss, that the emotional and psychological stress you are experiencing is taking a toll on your physical health. By addressing the toxic relationship and seeking help to heal the emotional wounds, you can also begin to restore your physical well-being.

Self-Reflection Questions

1. Have you noticed any changes in your physical health since being in this relationship, such as increased headaches, fatigue, or digestive problems?

2. Do you find yourself feeling anxious, depressed, or emotionally drained more often than not?

3. Have you lost interest in activities you once enjoyed or withdrawn from friends and family?

4. Do you often feel like you're losing your sense of self or that your identity is becoming intertwined with your partner's?

5. Are you experiencing any symptoms of PTSD, such as flashbacks, nightmares, or difficulty in sleeping?

Transformative Exercises

1. **Body Scan Meditation:** Practice a body scan meditation to become more aware of the physical sensations in your body. Notice any areas of tension, pain, or discomfort, and breathe into them with kindness and compassion.

2. **Stress Reduction Techniques:** Explore various stress reduction techniques, such as yoga, deep breathing exercises, or spending time in nature. These practices can help calm your nervous system and promote relaxation.

3. **Journaling:** Write down your thoughts and feelings about the impact the toxic relationship has had on your emotional and physical well-being. This can help you process your emotions and gain clarity on the situation.

4. **Reconnect with Yourself:** Make a list of activities you used to enjoy before the relationship. Start incorporating these activities back into your life to rediscover your passions and reconnect with your authentic self.

Part II: Reclaiming Your Power and Setting Boundaries

Chapter 4: Unmasking Your Inner Strength

In a toxic relationship, it's easy to lose sight of who you truly are. Like a precious gem buried beneath layers of dirt and grime, your inner strength and unique brilliance become obscured, hidden from your own view. But just as a skilled jeweler can uncover the hidden beauty of a gem, you too can rediscover the incredible strength that lies within you.

This chapter is your invitation to embark on a journey of self-discovery, a quest to unearth the treasures that have been buried beneath the weight of toxicity. It's a chance to peel back the layers of self-doubt and insecurity, revealing the radiant core of your being. By identifying your strengths and values, you'll gain a deeper understanding of who you are, what you stand for, and what you truly deserve in your relationships.

The first step on this journey is to shed the labels and limiting beliefs that have been imposed upon you by others. Perhaps you've been told that you're too sensitive, too needy, or not good enough. Maybe you've internalized these messages, believing them to be true. But it's time to challenge these narratives and rewrite your own story.

Start by asking yourself some powerful questions. What are you passionate about? What makes you feel alive and excited? What are your unique talents and abilities? What values do you hold dear? Take some time to reflect on these questions, journaling your thoughts and insights. As you delve deeper into your inner world, you'll begin to uncover the hidden gems of your personality.

Another way to identify your strengths is to reflect on your past accomplishments. What challenges have you overcome? What goals have you achieved? What obstacles have you surmounted? By acknowledging your past successes, you can tap into the resilience and resourcefulness that lies within you. Remember, you are capable of so much more than you may realize.

Once you've identified your strengths and values, it's time to start building your self-esteem. This is not about becoming arrogant or conceited. It's about recognizing your inherent worth and treating yourself with kindness and respect. It's about believing that you deserve to be loved, cherished, and treated with dignity.

One powerful way to build self-esteem is through positive affirmations. These are simple statements that you repeat to yourself, such as "I am worthy of love," "I am capable and strong," or "I am enough." By repeating these affirmations daily, you can start to reprogram your subconscious mind and cultivate a more positive self-image.

Another effective way to boost your self-esteem is to practice self-care. This means taking care of your physical, emotional, and mental well-being. It could involve anything from eating nourishing foods and exercising regularly to spending time in nature or pursuing a hobby you love. When you prioritize your own well-being, you send a powerful message to yourself and others that you are valuable and deserving of care.

Self-compassion is a viable recipe in rebuilding your depketed self-esteem. This means treating yourself with the same kindness and understanding that you would offer to a dear friend. It means acknowledging your imperfections and mistakes without judgment, and recognizing that you are human and therefore fallible. By practicing self-compassion, you can cultivate a more loving and accepting relationship with yourself.

You can practice self-compassion is through mindfulness meditation. This involves focusing your attention on the present moment without judgment. As you become more aware of your thoughts and feelings, you can start to cultivate a sense of inner peace and acceptance. You can also try writing a self-compassionate letter to yourself, acknowledging your struggles and offering yourself words of encouragement and support.

Rediscovering Your Worth

In the aftermath of a toxic relationship, it's easy to feel like you've lost a part of yourself. The constant criticism, manipulation, and devaluation can leave you feeling worthless and unlovable. But it's important to remember that your worth is not determined by anyone else. It's inherent, unchanging, and infinite.

Rediscovering your worth is a journey of self-love and acceptance. It's about recognizing the unique qualities that make you special, the strengths and talents that make you shine. It's about embracing your imperfections and loving yourself unconditionally, just as you are.

Start by making a list of all the things you love about yourself. It could be your kindness, your sense of humor, your creativity, or your intelligence. Write down everything that comes to mind, no matter how small or insignificant it may seem. As you read over your list, you'll be reminded of all the wonderful qualities that make you worthy of love and respect.

Next, challenge the negative beliefs that have been ingrained in you by your toxic partner. Every time you catch yourself thinking something negative about yourself, replace it with a positive affirmation. For example, instead of thinking "I'm not good enough," tell yourself "I am worthy of love and respect."

Surround yourself with positive influences. Spend time with people who uplift and support you, who see your worth and appreciate you for who you are. Avoid people who bring you down or make you feel bad about yourself.

Rediscovering your worth takes time, effort, and patience. But as you continue to nurture yourself and embrace your unique gifts, you'll begin to see yourself in a new light. You'll recognize the incredible worth that you possess, and you'll never again allow yourself to be treated as anything less than you deserve.

Cultivating Self-Compassion

Self-compassion is a gentle embrace, a soothing balm for the wounds inflicted by toxic relationships. It's the antidote to the harsh inner critic that tells you you're not good enough, not worthy of love, not deserving of happiness. By cultivating self-compassion, you can start to heal those wounds and reclaim your sense of self-worth.

Imagine yourself as a dear friend who is going through a difficult time. How would you speak to them? Would you berate them for their mistakes? Would you criticize their every flaw? Of course not. You would offer them kindness, understanding, and support. You would remind them of their strengths and encourage them to be gentle with themselves. This is the essence of self-compassion.

Start by noticing the negative self-talk that often accompanies feelings of inadequacy or shame. When you catch yourself thinking "I'm such a failure" or "I'm not good enough," pause for a moment and take a deep breath. Then, try to reframe those thoughts in a more compassionate way. For example, instead of saying "I'm such a failure," you could say "I'm going through a difficult time, but I'm doing my best." Instead of saying "I'm not good enough," you could say "I am worthy of love and respect, just as I am."

Another way to cultivate self-compassion is to practice mindfulness. This involves paying attention to your thoughts and feelings without judgment. Notice the physical sensations in your body, the emotions that arise, and the thoughts that pass through your mind. Simply observe them without trying to change them. This can help you become more aware of your inner critic and develop a more compassionate relationship with yourself.

Self-compassion is not about self-indulgence or making excuses for your mistakes. It's about recognizing that you are human and therefore imperfect, and that's okay. It's about treating yourself with the same kindness and understanding that you would offer to others.

Self-Reflection Questions

1. What are the negative beliefs about yourself that you've internalized as a result of the toxic relationship?

2. When you look back on your past accomplishments, what strengths and resources do you see within yourself?

3. How do you typically talk to yourself when you make a mistake or experience a setback? Is it kind and supportive, or critical and judgmental?

4. What are some ways you can practice self-care and prioritize your own well-being?

5. What positive affirmations resonate with you and can help you challenge negative self-talk?

Transformative Exercises

1. **Strength Inventory:** Write down a list of your strengths, talents, and accomplishments. Include anything that makes you feel proud and confident. Refer to this list whenever you're feeling down on yourself.

2. **Self-Compassion Break:** When you notice negative self-talk, pause and take a few deep breaths. Remind yourself that you are human and deserving of compassion. Offer yourself words of kindness and encouragement, just as you would to a friend.

3. **Letter of Self-Love:** Write a letter to yourself expressing love, appreciation, and acceptance. Acknowledge your struggles and imperfections, but also celebrate your strengths and resilience.

4. **Positive Affirmation Practice:** Choose a few positive affirmations that resonate with you and repeat them daily. Write them down, say them out loud, or even create a visual reminder to keep them at the forefront of your mind.

5. **Self-Care Challenge:** Commit to practicing one act of self-care every day for a week. This could be anything from taking a bubble bath to reading a book to spending time in nature. Notice how these acts of self-care make you feel and how they contribute to your overall well-being.

Chapter 5: The Art of Setting Boundaries

Take your life as an imaginary beautiful house, am abode where you feel safe, loved, and respected. This house has doors and windows, allowing light and warmth to enter, but also providing a barrier against unwanted intrusions. These doors and windows are like the boundaries in your relationships, protecting your emotional and mental space while allowing healthy connections to flourish.

Boundaries are the invisible lines that define where you end and others begin. They are the limits you set on what you will and will not tolerate in your interactions with others. Healthy boundaries are essential for all types of relationships, whether it's with your partner, family, friends, or colleagues. They create a sense of safety and security, allowing you to express your needs and desires without fear of judgment or reprisal.

Without boundaries, relationships can become a chaotic free-for-all, where your needs are constantly trampled upon and your emotional well-being is neglected. You may find yourself saying yes when you really want to say no, sacrificing your own happiness to please others. You may feel resentful and taken advantage of, but powerless to change the dynamic.

Setting boundaries is an act of self-love and self-respect. It's about recognizing that your needs are just as important as anyone else's and that you have the right to protect your emotional and mental space. It's not about being selfish or shutting people out. It's about creating healthy, balanced relationships where everyone feels valued and respected.

So, how do you set healthy boundaries? The first step is to identify your needs and limits. What are the things that you will and will not tolerate in a relationship? What behaviors make you feel uncomfortable, disrespected, or taken advantage of? Once you have a clear understanding of your needs, you can start to communicate them to others.

This can be a challenging step for many people, especially those who have been conditioned to prioritize others' needs above their own. You may fear that setting boundaries will damage your relationships or make you seem selfish. But remember, healthy relationships are built on mutual respect and understanding. When you communicate your boundaries clearly and assertively, you are actually strengthening your relationships by creating a foundation of trust and open communication.

When communicating your boundaries, it's important to be clear, direct, and specific. Avoid vague statements like "I need space" or "Don't do that." Instead, say something like "I need some time alone to recharge" or "I don't appreciate it when you raise your voice at me. Please speak to me calmly." By being specific, you leave no room for misinterpretation and ensure that your message is received loud and clear.

Enforcing your boundaries is just as important as setting them. This means holding firm when your boundaries are tested and not backing down even if someone pushes back or tries to guilt-trip you. Remember, you have the right to say no and to protect your emotional well-being. It may not always be easy, but standing your ground is essential for maintaining healthy relationships.

Consistency is key when it comes to enforcing boundaries. If you allow someone to cross your boundaries once, they are more likely to do it again. By consistently upholding your boundaries, you are sending a clear message that you are not to be messed with.

As you grow and evolve, your needs and limits may change. It's important to regularly check in with yourself and adjust your boundaries accordingly. This may involve having difficult conversations with loved ones, but it's essential for maintaining healthy relationships and protecting your well-being.

A lot of people misconstrue the ideal behind setting boundaries to mean controlling others. It's about taking control of your own life and creating a space where you feel safe, loved, and respected. It's about honoring your own needs and desires, while also respecting the needs and desires of others. By setting healthy boundaries, you can create relationships that are truly fulfilling and enriching, relationships that bring you joy and support rather than pain and depletion.

Defining Healthy Boundaries

Healthy boundaries act as the sturdy fence around your emotional garden, keeping the weeds of disrespect and manipulation at bay while allowing the sunshine of love and respect to nourish your soul. They are not rigid walls meant to shut people out, but rather flexible barriers that define your personal space and protect your well-being.

Imagine these boundaries as a set of personalized rules, tailored to your unique needs and preferences. They dictate what you are comfortable with and what you are not, what you will accept and what you will not tolerate in your relationships. They are like the terms and conditions of your emotional contract, ensuring that you are treated with respect, kindness, and consideration.

Healthy boundaries can be physical, emotional, or even digital. They can range from simple things like not answering the phone during dinner to more complex issues like refusing to engage in conversations that make you feel uncomfortable. The key is to identify what works for you and to communicate these boundaries clearly and assertively to others.

It's important to remember that healthy boundaries are not about controlling others. They are about taking control of your own life and creating a space where you feel safe, loved, and respected. By defining your boundaries and communicating them effectively, you are empowering yourself to say yes to the things that bring you joy and fulfillment and no to the things that drain your energy and compromise your well-being.

Some of the examples of healthy boundaries you might want to keep in check for your relationships are:

- **Physical boundaries:** This could involve not allowing others to touch you without your consent, setting limits on physical affection, or refusing to engage in sexual activity that makes you uncomfortable.

- **Emotional boundaries:** This could involve not allowing others to criticize or belittle you, setting limits on how much emotional energy you are willing to give, or refusing to engage in conversations that are hurtful or draining.

- **Digital boundaries:** This could involve setting limits on how much time you spend on social media, not responding to texts or emails after a certain hour, or unfriending or blocking people who post negative or triggering content.

Remember, setting healthy boundaries is an ongoing process. It takes time and practice to learn how to communicate your needs effectively and to stand your ground when your boundaries are tested. But with persistence and self-compassion, you can create a life where your boundaries are respected and your well-being is protected.

Communicating Your Boundaries Effectively

Communicating your boundaries effectively is an art, to ensure your of assertiveness, respect, and clarity. It's about expressing your needs and limits in a way that is both firm and compassionate, ensuring that your message is heard and understood.

Start by choosing the right time and place to have the conversation. Avoid bringing up sensitive topics when emotions are running high or when you're feeling rushed or distracted. Instead, find a quiet, private space where you can both focus on the conversation without interruptions.

When expressing your boundaries, use "I" statements to focus on your own feelings and needs. For example, instead of saying "You always interrupt me," you could say "I feel frustrated when I'm interrupted. I would appreciate it if you could let me finish my thoughts." This approach avoids blaming or accusing the other person, making it more likely that they will be receptive to your message.

Be clear and direct in your communication. Avoid vague statements or beating around the bush. State your boundaries clearly and concisely, leaving no room for misinterpretation. For example, instead of saying "I need some space," you could say "I need some time alone this evening to recharge. I'll be available to talk tomorrow."

It's also important to be assertive in your communication. This doesn't mean being aggressive or confrontational. It simply means standing up for yourself and your needs in a confident and respectful way. Use a calm, even tone of voice, maintain eye contact, and avoid apologizing for your boundaries. Remember, you have the right to set limits on what you will and will not tolerate.

Be prepared for pushback. Not everyone will be happy when you start setting boundaries. Some people may try to guilt-trip you, manipulate you, or dismiss your needs. But don't let this deter you. Stand your ground and reiterate your boundaries calmly and firmly. Remember, you are not responsible for their reactions, only for communicating your needs in a healthy and respectful way.

Effective communication is a two-way street. Listen to the other person's perspective, even if you don't agree with it. Try to understand their point of view and acknowledge their feelings. This doesn't mean you have to change your boundaries, but it can help to de-escalate the situation and create a more open and honest dialogue.

Self-Reflection Questions

1. What are your personal needs and limits in relationships? What behaviors do you find unacceptable or disrespectful?

2. Have you been clear and assertive in communicating your boundaries to others? If not, what has held you back?

3. How do you typically respond when someone pushes back against your boundaries? Do you stand your ground or give in?

4. Are there any areas in your life where you need to set stronger boundaries? What steps can you take to establish and enforce them?

5. How do you think setting and maintaining healthy boundaries can improve your relationships and overall well-being?

Transformative Exercises

1. **Boundary Inventory:** Take some time to reflect on your relationships and identify areas where you need to set or strengthen boundaries. Write down specific examples of behaviors you will no longer tolerate.

2. **"I" Statement Practice:** Practice using "I" statements to communicate your boundaries clearly and assertively. For example, instead of saying "You're always late," try saying "I feel disrespected when you're late. Please be on time in the future."

3. **Role-Playing:** Enlist a trusted friend or family member to role-play different scenarios where you need to communicate and enforce your boundaries. This can help you build confidence and practice assertiveness.

4. **Visualization:** Imagine yourself setting a boundary with someone who has previously pushed back. Visualize yourself remaining calm, assertive, and unwavering in your resolve. This can help you prepare for real-life situations where you need to stand your ground.

5. **Self-Affirmation:** Write down positive affirmations that remind you of your right to set boundaries and your worthiness of respect. Repeat these affirmations daily to reinforce your self-confidence and resolve.

Chapter 6: Dealing with Resistance and Backlash

Setting boundaries is a courageous act, a declaration of self-worth and a refusal to be a doormat any longer. However, it's not always a smooth journey. When you start asserting your needs and saying "no" to things that don't align with your values, you may encounter resistance and backlash from those who are accustomed to your compliance. This can be a challenging and even disheartening experience, but it's important to remember that it's a natural part of the process.

Think of it like a plant pushing through the soil, reaching for the sunlight. As it grows, it encounters obstacles – rocks, roots, and other barriers. But with persistence and determination, it finds a way to break through, eventually reaching its full potential. Similarly, when you set boundaries, you may face resistance from those who are threatened by your newfound assertiveness. But by staying true to yourself and your needs, you can overcome these obstacles and create a life that is authentic and fulfilling.

One common form of resistance is manipulation. Toxic individuals often use guilt trips, passive-aggressive tactics, and emotional blackmail to get their way. They may try to make you feel guilty for setting boundaries, accusing you of being selfish or uncaring. They may play the victim, claiming that your boundaries are hurting them. Or they may try to manipulate your emotions by threatening to withdraw their love or support.

The key to dealing with manipulation is to recognize it for what it is. Don't fall for their tactics or let them make you feel guilty for prioritizing your own well-being. Stay calm and assertive, reiterating your boundaries clearly and firmly. Remember, you have the right to say no and to protect your emotional space.

Another common form of resistance is gaslighting. This is a manipulative tactic where someone tries to make you doubt your own sanity or perception of reality. They may deny saying or doing things that you clearly remember, or they may accuse you of being oversensitive or imagining things. Gaslighting can be incredibly confusing and disorienting, leaving you feeling unsure of yourself and your own judgment.

The best way to deal with gaslighting is to trust your instincts. If something feels off, it probably is. Don't let anyone make you question your own reality. Keep a journal of your interactions, documenting any instances of gaslighting. This can help you see patterns of behavior and remind you of your own truth.

Sometimes, the resistance you encounter may come from loved ones who are genuinely concerned about you. They may worry that your boundaries are pushing them away or that you're changing in a way they don't understand. It's important to have open and honest conversations with these individuals, explaining why you're setting boundaries and how it's benefiting your well-being. Reassure them that you still care about them and value their relationship, but that you need to prioritize your own needs in order to be the best version of yourself.

When you want to set boundaries, be aware that it is not about cutting people out of your life. It's about creating healthier, more balanced relationships where everyone feels respected and valued. It's about learning to say yes to the things that truly matter to you and no to the things that don't.

As you continue on your journey from doormat to delightful, embrace the challenges that come with setting boundaries. View them as opportunities for growth and self-discovery. Remember, you are not alone in this journey. There are countless others who have walked this path before you, and there are resources available to support you along the way.

Strategies for Handling Manipulation and Guilt Trips

Manipulators and guilt-trippers are like skilled puppeteers, pulling on your emotional strings to get what they want. Their tactics can be subtle and insidious, making it difficult to recognize them for what they are. But with awareness and practice, you can learn to cut those strings and reclaim your power.

One common tactic is the guilt trip. The manipulator may try to make you feel responsible for their happiness or well-being, implying that you're a bad person if you don't comply with their demands. They may use phrases like "If you really loved me, you would..." or "You're always so selfish." The key to handling guilt trips is to recognize that you are not responsible for their emotions. You are not obligated to sacrifice your own needs to make them happy. It's okay to say no and to prioritize your own well-being.

A manipulator may employ the tactics of playing the victim. The manipulator may exaggerate their problems or downplay your concerns, making you feel guilty for not giving them enough attention or support. They may use phrases like "You never listen to me" or "I'm the only one who cares about this." The key to dealing with this tactic is to validate their feelings while also asserting your own. You can say something like "I hear that you're feeling upset, but I also need to take care of myself."

Manipulators may also try to isolate you from your support system. They may criticize your friends and family, making you feel like you can only rely on them. They may also try to control your time and activities, limiting your contact with others. The key to resisting this tactic is to maintain your connections with loved ones. Don't let anyone isolate you from your support system. Reach out to your friends and family for help and encouragement.

Finally, remember that you are not responsible for fixing the manipulator's problems. They are responsible for their own happiness and well-being. Don't let them guilt you into taking on their burdens. It's okay to set boundaries and prioritize your own needs.

When you are able to recognize these tactics and learned to stand up for yourself, you can break free from the manipulator's control and reclaim your power. You are not a doormat, but a strong and capable individual who deserves to be treated with respect.

Staying Firm in the Face of Pressure

Staying firm in the face of pressure is a testament to your newfound strength and resilience. When you encounter resistance to your boundaries, it's easy to feel overwhelmed and tempted to give in. The guilt trips, emotional blackmail, and manipulative tactics can be relentless, chipping away at your resolve. But remember, you are not a doormat anymore. You are a strong, capable individual who deserves to be treated with respect.

The key to staying firm is to remember why you set these boundaries in the first place. Think about the emotional and psychological toll the toxic relationship took on you. Recall the feelings of resentment, frustration, and depletion. This can help you stay focused on your goals and resist the temptation to back down.

Another helpful strategy is to have a support system in place. Surround yourself with people who believe in you and your right to set boundaries. Talk to a trusted friend, family member, or therapist about what you're going through. Their encouragement and support can be invaluable during challenging times.

When faced with pressure, take a deep breath and remind yourself of your worth. You are not obligated to please everyone, and you don't have to sacrifice your well-being for the sake of others. It's okay to say no and to prioritize your own needs.

It's also important to be prepared for the consequences of setting boundaries. Some people may not be able to handle your newfound assertiveness and may choose to distance themselves from you. This can be painful, but it's important to remember that not everyone is meant to be in your life. The people who truly care about you will respect your boundaries and support your growth.

Self-Reflection Questions

1. Have you ever experienced guilt trips or emotional blackmail when trying to set boundaries? How did it make you feel, and how did you respond?

2. Has anyone ever tried to gaslight you or make you doubt your own perception of reality? How did you handle it?

3. When faced with pressure to give in or compromise your boundaries, what strategies do you typically use to stay firm?

4. Who are the people in your life who support your boundaries and encourage your growth? How can you lean on them for support when facing resistance?

5. What are the potential consequences of setting boundaries, and how can you prepare yourself for them?

Transformative Exercises

1. **Guilt Trip Antidote:** Write a list of affirmations that counteract common guilt trip phrases. For example, if someone says "If you really loved me, you would…," you can respond with "I love you, and that's why I'm setting this boundary."

2. **Reality Check:** Keep a journal to document any instances of gaslighting or manipulation. Write down what happened,

how it made you feel, and what you can do to protect yourself in the future.

3. **Support Network:** Make a list of the people in your life who you can trust and rely on for support. Reach out to them regularly for encouragement and guidance.

4. **The Broken Record Technique:** Practice using the broken record technique, where you calmly and repeatedly state your boundary without engaging in arguments or justifications. This can be effective in deflecting manipulation and guilt trips.

5. **Self-Compassion Mantra:** Create a personal mantra that reminds you of your worth and your right to set boundaries. Repeat this mantra to yourself whenever you're feeling pressured or unsure of yourself.

Part III: Transforming or Leaving: Choosing Your Path

Chapter 7: Is Transformation Possible?

Amidst the wreckage of a toxic relationship, a glimmer of hope often flickers – the possibility of transformation. Can this wounded connection be healed? Can the poison be extracted, allowing a new, healthier bond to blossom in its place? The answer, like the complexities of human relationships themselves, is not a simple yes or no. It depends on a multitude of factors, a delicate dance of willingness, self-awareness, and commitment from both partners.

Transformation is not a magical cure-all, nor is it a guaranteed outcome. It requires a deep dive into the heart of the toxicity, a willingness to confront uncomfortable truths, and a commitment to change on both sides. It's a challenging path, fraught with obstacles and setbacks, but for those willing to embark on the journey, the rewards can be immense.

One of the key factors in determining whether transformation is possible is the willingness of both partners to acknowledge the toxicity and take responsibility for their role in creating it. This means recognizing the harmful patterns of behavior, the hurtful words, the dismissive actions that have eroded the foundation of the relationship. It means being honest with yourself and your partner about the pain you've caused and the changes you need to make.

This is often the most difficult step, as it requires a level of vulnerability and self-awareness that many people struggle with. It's easy to blame the other person, to point fingers and deflect responsibility. But true transformation can only begin when both partners are willing to look in the mirror and confront their own shortcomings.

Another crucial factor is the willingness of both partners to seek help and support. This could involve individual therapy, couples counseling, or support groups. A trained professional can provide a safe and neutral space for both partners to explore their feelings, communicate their needs, and develop healthier patterns of interaction.

Therapy can be particularly helpful in identifying the root causes of the toxic behavior. These could include childhood trauma, unresolved emotional issues, or underlying mental health conditions. By addressing these underlying issues, both partners can gain a deeper understanding of themselves and their relationship, paving the way for lasting change.

The change process itself is a gradual one, requiring patience, persistence, and a willingness to learn and grow. It involves unlearning old patterns of behavior and developing new, healthier ones. It may require setting boundaries, learning to communicate more effectively, and practicing empathy and compassion. It's a journey of self-discovery and healing, both individually and as a couple.

In some cases, transformation may not be possible. If one partner is unwilling to acknowledge the toxicity or take responsibility for their actions, then change is unlikely. Similarly, if one partner continues to engage in abusive or manipulative behavior, then the relationship is not safe or healthy.

There are also certain types of toxic relationships that are inherently difficult to transform. For example, relationships with narcissists or sociopaths are often characterized by a lack of empathy and remorse, making change nearly impossible. In these cases, the healthiest option may be to leave the relationship and focus on your own healing and well-being.

Deciding whether to stay and try to transform a toxic relationship or to leave is a deeply personal one. There is no right or wrong answer, and the best choice will vary depending on your individual circumstances. It's important to weigh the potential benefits of transformation against the risks of staying in a toxic environment.

It's also crucial to prioritize your own safety and well-being, seeking support from loved ones or professionals as needed.

Millions of people have struggled with toxic relationships, and there are countless resources available to help you heal and move forward. Whether you choose to stay and try to transform the relationship or to leave and start anew, remember that you are worthy of love, respect, and happiness. You deserve a relationship that nourishes and uplifts you, not one that leaves you feeling drained and depleted.

When Change is Realistic

In every toxic relationship, the question of transformation often looms large. Is it truly possible to mend the broken pieces and create something beautiful? While the path to healing is rarely easy, there are instances where change is not only possible but also realistic.

Transformation is most likely to occur when both partners are willing to acknowledge the toxicity and take ownership of their role in creating it. This requires a deep level of self-awareness and a willingness to confront uncomfortable truths about themselves and their behavior. It's about recognizing the patterns of hurt and pain that have been inflicted and expressing a genuine desire to break free from those cycles.

Open and honest communication is another crucial element for successful transformation. Both partners must be willing to express their needs, fears, and vulnerabilities in a safe and supportive environment. This involves active listening, empathy, and a commitment to understanding each other's perspectives. It's about creating a space where both partners feel heard, validated, and respected.

A willingness to seek professional help is often a sign that change is realistic. Couples therapy or individual counseling can provide the tools and guidance needed to navigate the complexities of a toxic relationship. A trained therapist can help identify the root causes of the toxicity, facilitate healthy communication, and teach coping mechanisms for dealing with conflict and triggers.

Change is also more likely when both partners are committed to personal growth and self-improvement. This means actively working on addressing any underlying issues that may be contributing to the toxicity, such as low self-esteem, unresolved trauma, or unhealthy coping mechanisms. It's about investing time and effort in personal development, whether through therapy, self-help resources, or other avenues of growth.

It's important to note that change is not a linear process. There will be setbacks and challenges along the way. Old patterns may resurface, and conflicts may arise. But with patience, perseverance, and a commitment to healing, transformation is possible.

Self-Reflection Questions

1. Are both you and your partner willing to acknowledge the toxicity in the relationship and take responsibility for your individual roles?

2. Are you both open to seeking professional help, such as couples counseling or individual therapy, to address the underlying issues and develop healthier patterns of communication?

3. Are you both committed to personal growth and self-improvement, willing to put in the time and effort to address any underlying issues that may be contributing to the toxicity?

4. Do you both believe that change is possible and are you willing to work together to create a healthier and more fulfilling relationship?

5. What are your individual and shared visions for a healthier relationship? Are you both aligned in your goals and expectations?

Transformative Exercises

1. **Shared Vision Board:** Create a vision board together, representing the kind of relationship you both aspire to have. Include images, words, and phrases that embody your shared values, goals, and dreams.

2. **Weekly Check-Ins:** Schedule weekly check-ins to discuss your progress, challenges, and any areas where you need to work on communication or understanding.

3. **Individual Therapy:** Consider seeking individual therapy to address any personal issues that may be contributing to the toxicity in the relationship.

4. **Couples Counseling:** Engage in couples counseling to learn healthy communication skills, conflict resolution strategies, and ways to rebuild trust and intimacy.

5. **Appreciation Exercise:** Take turns expressing appreciation for each other, focusing on positive qualities and actions. This can help foster a more positive and supportive dynamic in the relationship.

Chapter 8: The Decision to Leave

The decision to leave a toxic relationship is never easy. It's a crossroads filled with conflicting emotions, doubts, and fears. On one hand, there's the lingering hope that things can change, the belief that love can conquer all. On the other hand, there's the undeniable pain, the constant feeling of being drained and diminished. It's a choice that requires courage, self-awareness, and a deep understanding of your own worth.

There's no one-size-fits-all answer to the question of when to leave. Every relationship is unique, and the decision to stay or go is a deeply personal one. However, there are certain signs that can indicate it's time to walk away. If you find yourself constantly walking on eggshells, afraid to say or do anything that might upset your partner, it's a red flag. If your partner consistently belittles, criticizes, or manipulates you, it's a sign of disrespect that should not be tolerated. If you feel drained, depressed, or anxious in the relationship, it's a clear indication that your well-being is being compromised.

Physical or emotional abuse is never acceptable and should be an immediate dealbreaker. If your partner is hurting you in any way, it's time to prioritize your safety and get out of the situation. Remember, you deserve to be treated with love, respect, and dignity.

Once you've made the decision to leave, it's important to have a plan in place. This will help you stay safe and minimize the emotional turmoil. Start by confiding in trusted friends or family members who can offer support and guidance. Let them know what you're going through and ask for their help in making arrangements for your departure.

If you feel unsafe or threatened, consider seeking professional help. There are many organizations and hotlines that can provide support and resources for victims of domestic violence or abuse. They can help you create a safety plan, find temporary housing, and access legal and financial assistance.

When leaving a toxic relationship, it's important to be prepared for a range of emotions. You may feel a sense of relief and liberation, but also sadness, anger, and guilt. It's normal to grieve the loss of the relationship, even if it was unhealthy. Allow yourself to feel these emotions, but don't let them consume you.

Remember, leaving is not a sign of failure. It's an act of courage and self-love. It's about choosing to prioritize your own well-being and create a life that is authentic and fulfilling. It's about saying goodbye to the toxicity and embracing a future filled with possibilities.

Once you've left the toxic relationship, it's important to focus on your healing and recovery. This may involve seeking therapy or counseling, joining a support group, or simply spending time with loved ones who can offer you comfort and encouragement. It's also important to take care of yourself physically and emotionally. Eat healthy foods, exercise regularly, get enough sleep, and engage in activities that bring you joy.

Remember, healing takes time, and it's okay to not be okay. Be patient with yourself and allow yourself to grieve the loss of the relationship. But also remember that you are strong and resilient. You have the power to overcome this challenge and create a life that is truly delightful.

Leaving a toxic relationship is not the end of your story. It's a new beginning, a chance to rediscover yourself and create a life that is filled with love, joy, and authenticity. It's a journey from doormat to delightful, a transformation that will empower you and inspire others.

Knowing When It's Time to Go

The decision to leave a toxic relationship is rarely clear-cut. It's often a gradual realization, a series of small moments that accumulate until you can no longer ignore the truth. It's the feeling of walking on eggshells, the constant knot in your stomach, the nagging voice in your head whispering, "This isn't right."

Sometimes, the signs are blatant – physical or emotional abuse, constant criticism, or blatant disrespect. Other times, they're more subtle – a gradual erosion of your self-esteem, a feeling of isolation, or a persistent sense of unease.

If you find yourself constantly making excuses for your partner's behavior, justifying their actions, or blaming yourself for their mistreatment, it's a red flag. If you feel like you're losing yourself in the relationship, sacrificing your own needs and desires to please your partner, it's a sign that your well-being is being compromised.

Pay attention to your gut feelings. If you feel like something is off, it probably is. Don't ignore that nagging feeling of unease or dismiss your intuition. Trust yourself and your instincts.

Ultimately, the decision to leave is a personal one. There is no right or wrong answer, and the timing will be different for everyone. But if you find yourself constantly questioning whether you should stay or go, it's a sign that you're already on the path to making a change.

Remember, you are not alone. There are people who care about you and want to support you. Reach out to trusted friends, family members, or professionals who can offer you guidance and help you navigate this difficult decision.

Leaving a toxic relationship is not a sign of weakness or failure. It's an act of courage and self-love. It's about choosing to prioritize your own well-being and create a life that is authentic and fulfilling.

Making a Safe and Empowered Exit

Leaving a toxic relationship safely is paramount. It's about strategically prioritizing your well-being above all else. If you feel threatened or fear for your safety, seek help immediately. Reach out to trusted friends, family, or professionals who can provide support and guidance.

Creating a safe exit plan involves careful consideration and preparation. Start by gathering important documents like your passport, identification, financial records, and any evidence of abuse or threats. Secure a safe place to stay, whether it's with a loved one or at a shelter. If you have children, consider their safety as well, ensuring they are protected and cared for during the transition.

Financially empowering yourself is crucial for a safe exit. If possible, open a separate bank account and start saving money discreetly. Research available resources for financial assistance and legal aid. Seek advice from professionals who can guide you through the legal and financial aspects of leaving the relationship.

Self-Reflection Questions

1. What are the specific signs in your relationship that make you question whether it's time to leave?

2. Do you often find yourself making excuses for your partner's behavior or blaming yourself for their mistreatment?

3. Have you been ignoring your gut feeling or intuition about the relationship? What is it telling you?

4. Who are the trusted people in your life you can confide in and seek support from during this process?

5. What steps can you take to create a safe exit plan and ensure your well-being?

Transformative Exercises

1. **Journaling Exercise:** Write a letter to your past self, before you entered the toxic relationship. Offer advice, warnings, and words of encouragement.

2. **Safety Planning:** Create a detailed safety plan that includes a safe place to stay, emergency contacts, and a list of important documents to take with you.

3. **Financial Assessment:** Review your financial situation and explore options for financial independence, such as opening a separate bank account or seeking financial assistance.

4. **Support Network:** Reach out to trusted friends, family members, or professionals for support and guidance. Consider joining a support group for individuals leaving toxic relationships.

5. **Self-Affirmation Practice:** Write down positive affirmations that remind you of your strength, courage, and worthiness of love and respect. Repeat these affirmations daily to reinforce your self-belief and resilience.

Chapter 9: Healing and Recovery

Leaving a toxic relationship is akin to emerging from a dark tunnel into the blinding light of day. While the relief of escaping the toxicity is immense, the journey towards healing and recovery can be arduous and emotionally charged. Like a wounded warrior returning from battle, you may bear scars, both visible and invisible, that require time and care to mend.

The path to healing is not a linear one. It's a winding road with twists and turns, ups and downs. It's a journey of rediscovering yourself, rebuilding your self-esteem, and finding joy in life once again. While the process may seem daunting, remember that you are not alone. Countless others have walked this path before you, emerging stronger and more resilient than ever before.

One of the first steps on the road to recovery is acknowledging and understanding the stages of grief. Just as you would grieve the loss of a loved one, leaving a toxic relationship also involves a period of mourning. You may experience a range of emotions, from sadness and anger to guilt and confusion. It's important to allow yourself to feel these emotions without judgment. Don't try to rush the healing process or suppress your feelings. Instead, acknowledge them, embrace them, and allow them to flow through you.

Denial is often the first stage of grief. You may find yourself unable to accept that the relationship is truly over, clinging to the hope that things can still be salvaged. You may even try to rationalize your ex-partner's behavior, blaming yourself for the problems in the relationship. This is a natural defense mechanism, a way to protect yourself from the pain of loss. But it's important to move through this stage and accept the reality of the situation.

Anger is another common emotion experienced during the grieving process. You may feel rage towards your ex-partner for the hurt they caused you, or you may direct your anger inwards, blaming yourself for not seeing the warning signs sooner. It's important to express this anger in healthy ways, such as talking to a therapist, journaling, or engaging in physical activity.

Bargaining is a stage where you may try to negotiate with yourself or a higher power, hoping to change the outcome of the situation. You may find yourself thinking "If only I had been more patient" or "If only I had tried harder." But it's important to remember that you did the best you could with the information and resources you had at the time.

Depression is a natural part of the grieving process. You may feel overwhelmed by sadness, hopelessness, and a loss of interest in activities you once enjoyed. It's important to reach out for support during this time, whether it's from friends, family, or a therapist. Don't isolate yourself or try to tough it out alone.

Acceptance is the final stage of grief, where you come to terms with the end of the relationship and begin to move forward. You may still feel sadness or regret, but you also begin to see the possibilities for a brighter future. You start to focus on your own healing and well-being, and you may even find yourself feeling grateful for the lessons learned from the experience.

As you move through the stages of grief, it's important to focus on rebuilding your self-esteem. This may involve challenging the negative beliefs you internalized during the relationship, such as "I'm not good enough" or "I don't deserve happiness." Replace these negative thoughts with positive affirmations, such as "I am worthy of love" or "I am strong and capable."

Surround yourself with supportive people who believe in you and your ability to heal. Spend time with friends and family who uplift and encourage you. Consider joining a support group or seeking therapy to help you process your emotions and develop healthy coping mechanisms.

Rediscovering joy in life is an essential part of the healing process. Engage in activities that bring you pleasure, whether it's spending time in nature, pursuing a hobby, or simply relaxing with a good book. Reconnect with old friends or make new ones. Find activities that make you laugh and remind you of the joy that exists in the world.

Remember, healing is a journey, not a destination. It takes time, effort, and a willingness to face your pain head-on. But with patience and perseverance, you can emerge from the ashes of a toxic relationship stronger, wiser, and more resilient than ever before.

Grieving the Loss of the Relationship

The end of a toxic relationship, even one that brought you pain, is a loss. It's the loss of a shared history, of dreams and promises, of a future that will never be. It's natural to grieve this loss, even if you know deep down that leaving was the right decision. This grief can manifest in various ways, from sadness and anger to confusion and denial.

Allow yourself to feel these emotions. Don't try to suppress them or pretend they don't exist. Acknowledge your pain, honor your feelings, and give yourself permission to grieve. Cry if you need to, scream if you must, write down your thoughts and feelings in a journal. This is a time for self-care and compassion. Be kind to yourself, nurture your body and soul, and surround yourself with supportive people who can offer a listening ear and a shoulder to cry on.

Remember, grief is a process, not an event. There's no set timeline for healing, and everyone experiences it differently. Some days you may feel strong and hopeful, while other days you may feel overwhelmed by sadness and despair. This is all normal and part of the healing journey.

Don't be afraid to seek professional help if you're struggling to cope. A therapist can provide a safe space for you to process your emotions, offer guidance and support, and help you develop healthy coping mechanisms.

Remember, grieving the loss of a toxic relationship is not a sign of weakness. It's a testament to your capacity for love, your resilience, and your ability to heal. By allowing yourself to grieve, you are taking an important step towards reclaiming your joy and embracing a brighter future.

Rebuilding Your Life After Toxicity

Rebuilding your life after a toxic relationship is like piecing together a shattered mosaic. It takes time, patience, and a gentle touch. Each piece, representing a different aspect of your life, needs to be carefully examined, cleaned, and then reassembled into a new, more beautiful whole.

Start by reassessing your priorities. What truly matters to you? What are your passions, your dreams, your goals? During the toxic relationship, your own needs and desires may have been neglected or suppressed. Now is the time to rediscover them and make them a priority.

Reconnect with your support system. Reach out to friends and family who can offer love, encouragement, and a listening ear. Consider joining a support group or seeking therapy to help you process your emotions and develop healthy coping mechanisms. Surrounding yourself with positive and supportive people can make a world of difference in your healing journey.

Create new routines and rituals that nourish your soul. This could involve anything from practicing yoga or meditation to spending time in nature or pursuing a creative hobby. Fill your life with activities that bring you joy and help you reconnect with your authentic self.

Don't be afraid to try new things and step outside of your comfort zone. This is a time for growth and self-discovery. Take a class, learn a new skill, or travel to a new place. Embrace the unknown and open yourself up to new possibilities.

Self-Reflection Questions

1. What emotions are you experiencing as you grieve the loss of the toxic relationship? Are you allowing yourself to feel these emotions without judgment?

2. What negative beliefs about yourself did you internalize during the relationship? How can you challenge these beliefs and replace them with positive affirmations?

3. Who are the supportive people in your life who can offer you comfort and encouragement during this time? Have you reached out to them for support?

4. What activities bring you joy and help you reconnect with your authentic self? How can you incorporate more of these activities into your daily life?

5. What new goals or dreams do you have for your future? What steps can you take to start moving towards them?

Transformative Exercises

1. **Grief Journaling:** Set aside some time each day to write down your thoughts and feelings about the loss of the relationship. Allow yourself to express your sadness, anger, guilt, or any other emotions that arise.

2. **Affirmation Practice:** Write down positive affirmations that counteract the negative beliefs you internalized during the relationship. Repeat these affirmations daily to reprogram your subconscious mind and build self-esteem.

3. **Support System Connection:** Make a list of the people in your life who you can trust and rely on for support. Reach out to them regularly for encouragement, advice, and a listening ear.

4. **Joyful Activities List:** Create a list of activities that bring you joy and fulfillment. Make a commitment to engage in at least one of these activities every day.

5. **Goal Setting:** Set realistic and achievable goals for your future. Break down these goals into smaller steps and create a plan for achieving them. This can give you a sense of purpose and direction as you rebuild your life.

Part IV: Building Healthy and Delightful Relationships

Chapter 10: Attracting Healthy Connections

Oftentimes, coming out of a toxic relationship, the path towards attracting healthy connections may seem daunting.. Yet, this journey is not about luck or chance, but a conscious shift in mindset, a deliberate cultivation of self-love, and a commitment to choosing partners who uplift and empower you.

Think of your heart as a magnet, attracting the energy that you radiate outwards. If you're emitting vibrations of insecurity, desperation, or low self-worth, you're more likely to draw in partners who mirror those same qualities. However, when you cultivate self-love, radiate confidence, and set healthy boundaries, you become a beacon for healthy, fulfilling connections.

The first step in this transformation is to shift your mindset. Instead of focusing on what you lack or what's wrong with you, focus on your strengths, your values, and your unique gifts. Embrace your imperfections and celebrate your individuality. Remember, you are worthy of love and respect, just as you are.

Self-love is not about vanity or narcissism. It's about recognizing your inherent worth and treating yourself with kindness and compassion. It's about prioritizing your own needs and well-being, setting healthy boundaries, and saying no to things that don't align with your values. When you love and respect yourself, you naturally attract others who do the same.

Self-care is an essential component of self-love. It's about nurturing your body, mind, and spirit. This could involve anything from eating nourishing foods and exercising regularly to spending time in nature or pursuing a hobby you love. When you take care of yourself, you radiate a vibrant energy that is attractive to others.

Choosing compatible partners is another key factor in attracting healthy connections. This means looking beyond the initial spark of attraction and considering whether your values, goals, and lifestyles align. It also means paying attention to how you feel when you're around them. Do they uplift and inspire you, or do they drain your energy and make you feel insecure?

A healthy partner will respect your boundaries, support your dreams, and encourage your personal growth. They will celebrate your successes and offer a shoulder to lean on during challenging times. They will communicate openly and honestly, resolving conflicts in a constructive way. And most importantly, they will love and accept you for who you truly are.

It's also important to be mindful of red flags in potential partners. If someone consistently disrespects your boundaries, belittles your accomplishments, or tries to control your actions, these are signs of a toxic personality that should not be ignored. Trust your instincts and don't settle for anything less than a healthy, respectful, and loving relationship.

Attracting healthy connections is a journey of self-discovery and personal growth. It's about shedding old patterns and beliefs that no longer serve you and embracing a new, empowering mindset. It's about recognizing your worth and choosing partners who reflect that worth back to you. It's about creating a life filled with love, joy, and authentic connection.

Shifting Your Mindset

Shifting your mindset after a toxic relationship is like changing the channel on a TV stuck on a static-filled station. It's about tuning into a new frequency, one that broadcasts messages of self-worth, abundance, and possibility.

This starts with recognizing the negative thought patterns that may have taken root during your toxic relationship. These could be beliefs like "I'm not good enough," "I'm unlovable," or "I always attract the wrong people." Once you identify these thoughts, challenge them. Are they really true? Or are they remnants of the toxicity you've left behind?

Replace these negative thoughts with positive affirmations that resonate with your newfound strength and resilience. Instead of "I'm not good enough," try "I am worthy of love and respect." Instead of "I'm unlovable," say "I am lovable and deserving of happiness." These affirmations may feel awkward at first, but with repetition, they can start to rewire your brain and create a more positive self-image.

Another way to shift your mindset is to focus on gratitude. Instead of dwelling on what went wrong in your past relationship, focus on what you've learned and how you've grown. Be grateful for the opportunity to start anew and create a healthier, happier future for yourself.

Remember, your mindset is a powerful tool. When you choose to focus on the positive and embrace a mindset of abundance, you open yourself up to a world of possibilities. You attract healthier relationships, you see opportunities where you once saw obstacles, and you begin to create a life that is truly delightful.

Practicing Self-Love and Self-Care

Practicing self-love and self-care isn't a selfish indulgence, but a vital step towards healing and attracting healthy connections. After enduring a toxic relationship, your emotional reserves may be depleted, your self-worth battered, and your spirit yearning for nourishment. Like a delicate plant starved of sunlight and water, you need to tend to your own needs before you can bloom again.

Self-love begins with recognizing your inherent worth, independent of any relationship. It's about accepting yourself, flaws and all, and treating yourself with kindness and compassion. This means silencing the inner critic that whispers doubts and insecurities, replacing those negative thoughts with affirmations of self-love and acceptance. It means celebrating your strengths, acknowledging your accomplishments, and forgiving yourself for any perceived shortcomings.

Self-care is the tangible expression of self-love. It's about prioritizing your well-being, both physically and emotionally. This could involve simple acts like taking a relaxing bath, indulging in a favorite hobby, or spending time in nature. It could also mean setting boundaries with others, saying no to commitments that drain your energy, and making time for activities that recharge your soul.

When you prioritize self-care, you're sending a powerful message to yourself and the world that you value your own well-being. You're also creating a solid foundation for attracting healthy relationships. When you're happy and fulfilled within yourself, you naturally radiate a positive energy that draws others towards you.

Self-Reflection Questions

1. What negative thought patterns have you noticed since leaving your toxic relationship? How can you challenge and reframe these thoughts?

2. What are your unique strengths, values, and gifts? How can you celebrate and express them more fully in your life?

3. What are some simple self-care practices that you can incorporate into your daily routine to nourish your mind, body, and spirit?

4. How can you prioritize your own needs and well-being without feeling guilty or selfish?

5. What steps can you take to cultivate a more positive and abundant mindset?

Transformative Exercises

1. **Affirmation Journal:** Write down positive affirmations that resonate with you and repeat them daily. This can help rewire your brain for self-love and acceptance.

2. **Gratitude Practice:** Each day, write down three things you're grateful for. This could include your strengths, your accomplishments, or simply the good things in your life.

3. **Self-Care Ritual:** Create a personalized self-care ritual that includes activities that nourish your mind, body, and soul. Make this ritual a regular part of your routine.

4. **Vision Board:** Create a vision board that represents the kind of life you want to create. Include images, words, and phrases that inspire and motivate you.

5. **Boundary Setting Exercise:** Identify areas in your life where you need to set stronger boundaries. Write down specific actions you can take to enforce these boundaries and protect your well-being.

Chapter 11: Nurturing Healthy Relationships

Healthy communication is the lifeblood of any thriving relationship. It's the bridge that connects two souls, allowing for the exchange of thoughts, feelings, and dreams. But communication is more than just exchanging words. It's about truly listening, understanding, and validating each other's perspectives. It's about expressing your needs and desires honestly and respectfully, while also being receptive to your partner's needs.

To cultivate healthy communication, start by practicing active listening. This means giving your undivided attention to your partner, focusing on their words and body language, and reflecting back what you hear to ensure understanding. Avoid interrupting, judging, or offering unsolicited advice. Instead, create a safe space where your partner feels heard and valued.

Expressing your needs and feelings openly and honestly is also essential for healthy communication. Don't bottle up your emotions or assume that your partner can read your mind. Instead, share your thoughts and feelings in a clear, direct, and respectful way. Use "I" statements to focus on your own experience, rather than blaming or accusing your partner. For example, instead of saying "You never listen to me," you could say "I feel hurt when I don't feel heard."

Mutual respect is the cornerstone of any healthy relationship. It's about valuing your partner's opinions, feelings, and boundaries, even when you disagree with them. It's about treating them with kindness, consideration, and compassion. It's about recognizing their autonomy and supporting their individual growth.

Respect is not about always agreeing or never arguing. It's about disagreeing in a respectful way, without resorting to insults, personal attacks, or manipulation. It's about valuing your partner's perspective, even if you don't share it. It's about creating a space where both of you can feel safe to express your opinions and be yourselves.

Trust is the glue that holds a relationship together. It's the belief that your partner has your best interests at heart, that they will be there for you through thick and thin, and that they will honor your commitments. Trust is built over time through consistent actions and open communication.

To build trust in your relationship, start by being trustworthy yourself. Keep your promises, be honest and transparent, and follow through on your commitments. Show your partner that you can be relied upon, both in good times and bad.

Communication is also crucial for building trust. Share your thoughts and feelings openly and honestly, even when it's difficult. Be willing to listen to your partner's perspective and validate their emotions. By fostering open communication, you create an environment where trust can flourish.

Intimacy is the deep connection that binds two souls together. It's the feeling of closeness, vulnerability, and shared experience. Intimacy can be physical, emotional, or spiritual, and it's an essential ingredient in any fulfilling relationship.

To cultivate intimacy in your relationship, start by creating opportunities for connection. This could involve setting aside regular time for date nights, engaging in shared activities, or simply cuddling up on the couch and talking. It's also important to be present and engaged in the moment, putting away distractions like phones and laptops.

Vulnerability is another key ingredient in intimacy. This means being willing to share your fears, insecurities, and dreams with your partner. It means letting down your guard and allowing yourself to be truly seen. By being vulnerable, you create a deeper level of connection and trust.

Strengthening your connection with your partner is an ongoing process. It requires effort, commitment, and a willingness to learn and grow together. Here are a few practical tips and exercises to help you nurture a healthy, fulfilling relationship:

- **Practice gratitude:** Take time each day to appreciate your partner and express your gratitude for their presence in your life.

- **Learn each other's love language:** Discover how your partner likes to receive love (e.g., words of affirmation, acts of service, gifts, quality time, physical touch) and make an effort to express your love in their preferred way.

- **Set aside time for fun and playfulness:** Don't let your relationship become all about work and responsibilities. Make time for laughter, adventure, and lightheartedness.

- **Celebrate each other's achievements:** Be your partner's biggest cheerleader, celebrating their successes and offering encouragement during challenging times.

A healthy relationship requires ongoing effort and a willingness to adapt and grow together. By cultivating healthy communication, mutual respect, trust, and intimacy, you can create a love that lasts a lifetime.

Effective Communication

Effective communication is the backbone of any healthy relationship, a bridge that connects two hearts and minds. It's the art of expressing your thoughts, feelings, and needs in a way that is both clear and compassionate, ensuring that your message is heard and understood. After escaping a toxic relationship where communication was likely fraught with manipulation and misunderstandings, learning to communicate effectively is a vital step in fostering healthy connections.

Imagine a dance, where two partners move in sync, their bodies flowing together in perfect harmony. Effective communication is like that dance, a delicate interplay of listening, speaking, and understanding. It's about being present in the moment, truly hearing what your partner is saying, and responding with empathy and respect.

Start by actively listening to your partner. This means putting aside distractions, focusing on their words and body language, and reflecting back what you hear to ensure understanding. Avoid interrupting, judging, or offering unsolicited advice. Instead, create a safe space where your partner feels heard and valued.

Expressing your own thoughts and feelings is just as important. Be clear, direct, and honest in your communication. Avoid passive-aggressive behavior or beating around the bush. Use "I" statements to focus on your own experience, rather than blaming or accusing your partner. For example, instead of saying "You always make me feel bad," you could say "I feel hurt when you say that."

Nonverbal communication is just as important as verbal communication. Pay attention to your tone of voice, facial expressions, and body language. Make eye contact, nod your head to show that you're listening, and offer reassuring touches when appropriate. These small gestures can go a long way in conveying warmth, understanding, and connection.

Mutual Respect and Support

Mutual respect and support are the sturdy pillars upon which a healthy relationship stands. Respect means valuing your partner's thoughts, feelings, and opinions, even when they differ from your own. It means listening attentively, speaking kindly, and refraining from belittling or demeaning remarks.

Support is the outstretched hand, always ready to offer encouragement, comfort, and a listening ear. It's about celebrating your partner's successes, empathizing with their struggles, and being their biggest cheerleader. It's about creating a safe space where they feel loved, accepted, and empowered to be their authentic selves.

In a healthy relationship, respect and support are a two-way street. Both partners give and receive these essential elements, fostering a sense of equality and mutual appreciation. This creates a strong foundation for trust, intimacy, and lasting love.

Self-Reflection Questions

1. How do you typically communicate with your partner? Are you an active listener, or do you tend to interrupt or offer unsolicited advice?

2. How comfortable are you expressing your needs and feelings openly and honestly? Do you feel safe to share your vulnerabilities with your partner?

3. How do you show respect to your partner? Do you value their opinions and boundaries, even when you disagree with them?

4. How do you offer support to your partner? Are you their biggest cheerleader, or do you tend to criticize or judge them?

5. What steps can you take to improve communication, respect, and support in your relationship?

Transformative Exercises

1. **Active Listening Challenge:** For one week, practice active listening with your partner. Focus on truly hearing their

words, reflecting back what you hear, and validating their feelings.

2. **"I" Statement Practice:** Make a conscious effort to use "I" statements when expressing your needs and feelings. This can help avoid blaming or accusing your partner and foster a more open and honest dialogue.

3. **Respectful Disagreement:** The next time you disagree with your partner, practice expressing your viewpoint respectfully and without judgment. Listen to their perspective and try to find common ground.

4. **Acts of Support:** Identify specific ways you can offer support to your partner, whether it's listening to their concerns, helping them with a task, or simply offering words of encouragement.

5. **Love Language Exchange:** Learn each other's love language and make a conscious effort to express your love and appreciation in ways that resonate with your partner.

Chapter 12: Maintaining Your Delightful Self

The journey from doormat to delightful is not a sprint but a marathon, a continuous evolution of self-discovery and personal growth. Like a butterfly emerging from its chrysalis, you have shed the weight of toxicity and embraced your true potential. But the metamorphosis doesn't end there. It's an ongoing process of learning, evolving, and becoming the most delightful version of yourself.

Embracing self-discovery is key to maintaining your newfound delight. It's about delving deeper into your passions, exploring your interests, and uncovering hidden talents. It's about challenging yourself to step outside your comfort zone and try new things. By continuously learning and growing, you expand your horizons, enrich your life, and become a more interesting and well-rounded individual.

Personal growth is not just about acquiring new knowledge or skills. It's also about cultivating self-awareness, understanding your strengths and weaknesses, and working towards becoming the best version of yourself. This could involve setting goals, practicing mindfulness, seeking therapy, or simply taking time for introspection and reflection.

By prioritizing personal growth, you not only enhance your own well-being but also attract positive energy into your life. Like a beacon of light, you attract people who are also on a path of growth and self-discovery. These are the individuals who will support and encourage you, who will challenge you to reach your full potential, and who will celebrate your successes alongside you.

Preventing future toxic relationships is another crucial aspect of maintaining your delightful self. While the scars of past wounds may linger, you can arm yourself with knowledge and awareness to avoid repeating the same patterns.

Start by recognizing the red flags of toxicity. These could include controlling behavior, constant criticism, emotional manipulation, or a lack of respect for your boundaries. If you notice these signs early on, don't ignore them. Trust your instincts and walk away from relationships that don't feel right.

Remember, you have the power to choose who you let into your life. Surround yourself with people who uplift and empower you, who celebrate your successes, and who support your dreams. These are the individuals who will nurture your growth and help you maintain a positive self-image.

Maintaining a positive self-image is essential for attracting healthy relationships. When you love and respect yourself, you naturally set a standard for how others should treat you. You won't tolerate disrespect, manipulation, or any behavior that diminishes your worth. Instead, you'll attract partners who see your value and cherish you for who you are.

Building a positive self-image takes time and effort. It involves challenging negative self-talk, practicing self-compassion, and celebrating your unique qualities. It also means surrounding yourself with positive influences, whether it's supportive friends and family, inspirational books and podcasts, or uplifting social media accounts.

Remember, your self-worth is not determined by your relationship status or anyone else's opinion of you. It's an inherent quality that exists within you, regardless of your circumstances. By cultivating self-love and embracing your own unique brilliance, you become a magnet for positive energy and healthy connections.

As you continue on your journey from doormat to delightful, remember that maintaining your newfound happiness and well-being is an ongoing process. It requires constant self-reflection, a willingness to learn and grow, and a commitment to setting healthy boundaries. But the rewards are immeasurable.

Ongoing Growth and Self-Discovery

Your journey from doormat to delightful is a testament to your resilience and capacity for growth. But the path to self-discovery doesn't end with escaping a toxic relationship. It's a lifelong adventure, a continuous unfolding of your true potential. Embrace this ongoing journey, for it's in the pursuit of growth that you'll truly flourish.

Don't settle for stagnation. Seek out new experiences, challenge yourself, and step outside your comfort zone. Learn a new skill, explore a different culture, or delve into a subject that piques your curiosity. Each new experience expands your horizons, enriches your life, and brings you closer to your authentic self.

Cultivate a thirst for knowledge and a hunger for personal development. Read books, attend workshops, listen to podcasts, and engage in conversations that inspire and challenge you. The more you learn, the more you grow.

Growth is not always comfortable. It often involves facing your fears, confronting your limitations, and embracing vulnerability. But it's in those moments of discomfort that true transformation occurs.

Embrace the challenges, for they are the stepping stones to a more fulfilling and authentic life.

As you continue on this journey of growth and self-discovery, remember that you are not alone. Surround yourself with a supportive community of friends, family, or mentors who believe in your potential and encourage your dreams. Seek guidance from therapists or coaches who can help you navigate challenges and unlock your full potential.

Most importantly, be kind to yourself. Growth takes time and effort, and setbacks are inevitable. Don't beat yourself up for mistakes or perceived failures. Instead, view them as opportunities for learning and growth. Celebrate your successes, no matter how small they may seem. And always remember, you are worthy of love, happiness, and a life filled with joy and fulfillment.

Preventing Future Toxicity

Preventing future toxicity is like cultivating a resilient garden. It's about nurturing healthy soil, planting strong seeds, and diligently weeding out any unwanted growth. Just as a gardener protects their plants from pests and diseases, you too can safeguard your emotional well-being by recognizing and avoiding toxic patterns.

One of the most effective ways to prevent future toxicity is to learn from your past experiences. Reflect on the red flags you may have missed in previous relationships. What were the early warning signs that you overlooked or dismissed? By understanding the patterns that led you to toxic relationships, you can become more aware of them in the future and make more informed choices.

Setting healthy boundaries is another crucial step in preventing future toxicity. Remember, your boundaries are your protectors, shielding you from emotional harm and ensuring that your needs are met. Don't be afraid to say no to things that don't align with your values or make you feel uncomfortable. Communicate your limits clearly and assertively, and don't be afraid to walk away from situations or relationships that feel toxic.

Surrounding yourself with positive and supportive people is also key to preventing future toxicity. Choose friends and partners who uplift and empower you, who celebrate your successes, and who respect your boundaries. Avoid people who drain your energy, criticize you constantly, or try to control your life.

Remember, you are worthy of love, respect, and healthy relationships. By learning from your past, setting boundaries, and choosing your company wisely, you can create a future filled with joy, fulfillment, and delightful connections.

Self-Reflection Questions

1. What new experiences or challenges can you embrace to foster your personal growth and self-discovery?

2. How can you actively seek out opportunities for learning and development in your life?

3. What are some negative thought patterns or limiting beliefs that may be hindering your growth? How can you challenge and reframe them?

4. Who are the positive and supportive people in your life who can encourage and uplift you on your journey? How can you cultivate deeper connections with them?

5. What steps can you take to be more mindful of red flags in potential partners and avoid repeating patterns of toxicity?

Transformative Exercises

1. **Growth Goals:** Set three specific, measurable, achievable, relevant, and time-bound (SMART) goals for your personal growth. This could involve learning a new skill, taking a course, or starting a new hobby.

2. **Gratitude Journal:** Each day, write down three things you are grateful for. This practice can help shift your focus to the positive aspects of your life and cultivate a sense of abundance.

3. **Self-Compassion Meditation:** Practice self-compassion meditation to cultivate a kinder and more accepting relationship with yourself. This can involve acknowledging your struggles without judgment and offering yourself words of encouragement and support.

4. **Positive Affirmation Ritual:** Create a daily ritual of repeating positive affirmations that resonate with you. This can help reprogram your subconscious mind and build self-esteem.

5. **Red Flag Review:** Reflect on past relationships and identify the red flags you missed or ignored. Make a list of these red flags and commit to being more mindful of them in future interactions.

Conclusion

Take a moment to reflect on the incredible journey you've taken. From the depths of a toxic relationship, you've emerged as a radiant being, filled with newfound strength, self-love, and resilience. You've shed the doormat label and embraced your own unique brilliance. You've learned to set boundaries, communicate your needs, and prioritize your well-being. You've discovered the power of self-compassion and learned to cultivate healthy, fulfilling connections.

Your transformation is a testament to the strength of the human spirit, a shining example of what's possible when we choose to rise above adversity. It's a reminder that even in the darkest of times, there is always hope for a brighter future.

But your journey doesn't end here. It's an ongoing process of growth, self-discovery, and empowerment. It's about continuing to nurture your inner strength, cultivating healthy relationships, and embracing a life of joy and fulfillment.

Your transformation is not just for you. It's a gift to the world. By sharing your story, you inspire others to break free from the chains of toxicity and reclaim their own power. You become a beacon of hope, a shining example of what's possible when we choose to love ourselves and set healthy boundaries.

Think of the ripple effect you can create. By sharing your journey, you may ignite a spark in someone else who is struggling in a toxic relationship. You may give them the courage to seek help, to set boundaries, to walk away from a situation that is no longer serving them. You may even inspire them to embark on their own journey of self-discovery and transformation.

Your story is a powerful reminder that we are not alone in our struggles. It's a testament to the resilience of the human spirit and the power of love to heal and transform. By sharing your experiences, you not only empower yourself but also empower others to break free from the chains of toxicity and create lives filled with joy, love, and authenticity.

So, celebrate your transformation. Share your story with others. Be a beacon of hope for those who are still struggling. And most importantly, continue to embrace your delightful self, for you are a gift to the world.

Let your journey be an inspiration to others. Share your triumphs and setbacks, your lessons learned, and your newfound wisdom. Be a voice for those who are still silenced by fear and self-doubt. By sharing your story, you create a ripple effect of healing and empowerment, touching countless lives and making the world a brighter place.

Your story matters. Your voice is powerful. And your journey is a testament to the resilience of the human spirit. So, step into the light, embrace your delight, and inspire others to do the same.